VOYAGES OF DISCOVERY

Explorers
of the Ancient World

Author Anthony Brierley

Series Editor Giovanni Caselli
Book Editor Penny Clarke

Created, designed and produced by
Studio Illibill, Florence, Italy

Illustrations by
Simone Boni, Lorenzo Cecchi,
Francesca D'Ottavi, Paola Ravaglia,
Claudia Saraceni, Thomas Trojer

Published by
PETER BEDRICK BOOKS
2112 Broadway
New York, NY 10023

Published by agreement with
Macdonald Young Books Ltd, England

Library of Congress Cataloging-in-
Publication Data

Brierley, Anthony.
    Explorers of the ancient world /
Anthony Brierley. – 1st American ed.
      p.   cm. – (Voyages of discovery)
    Includes index.
    Summary: Describes some of the
voyages of exploration made by ancient
Egyptians, Phoenicians, and Greeks as
long as four thousand years ago.
    ISBN 0-87226-485-8
    1. Explorers–Juvenile literature.
2. Discoveries in geography–Juvenile
literature. 3. Geography, Ancient–
Juvenile literature. [1 Discoveries in
geography. 2. Geography, Ancient.
3. Explorers.]   I Title.   II. Series.
G175.B714 1996   96–1261
910'.93–dc20   CIP
                            AC

00 99 98 97 96 1 2 3 4 5

Printed in Hong Kong

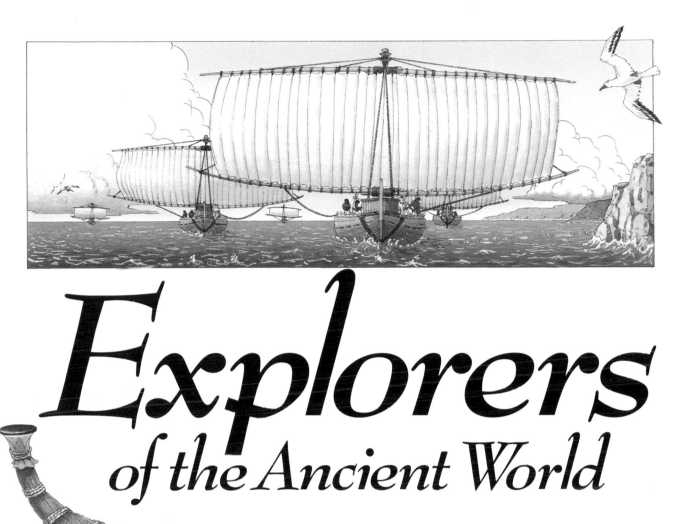

Explorers
of the Ancient World

Anthony Brierley

PETER BEDRICK BOOKS

NEW YORK

CONTENTS

THE EGYPTIANS sailed to the mysterious land of Punt around 1485 BC. They may have been there before, but this is the earliest voyage for which records have survived. Scenes of the voyage are carved on the walls of Queen Hatshepsut's burial temple. The voyagers brought back rare goods from Africa on the Queen's orders.

INTRODUCTION

The story of exploration goes back many, many thousands of years. Exploration began at the dawn of time, when people first moved into lands they did not know, ventured into uncharted waters, and stepped onto shores where, as far as they knew, no human had ever been. We know almost nothing about these first explorers and their journeys of discovery. They left no records, diaries or maps. Nor do we know anything about the boats in which they sailed on these dangerous voyages.

   The great voyages of exploration described in this book were made by the ancient Egyptians, Phoenicians and Greeks in the first and second millennia BC (between two and four thousand years ago). There are records of these early explorers and their voyages. Stories and pictures describing them have survived. Some of the pictures are shown in this book.

Explorers in the Ancient World

The map on these two pages shows the Mediterranean Sea and the surrounding lands in the 2000 years before the birth of Christ. During this time a number of great civilizations flourished around the Mediterranean. One of the earliest of these civilizations was in Egypt. It developed in the valley of the River Nile about 3000 BC. Egyptian rulers (pharaohs) sent a number of expeditions south to trade with African rulers.

Many centuries later, the Phoenicians developed a thriving sea trade. Their ships sailed all over the Mediterranean from the area that is now modern Lebanon.

The ancient Greeks, another great civilization of this time, faced a land shortage. To solve the problem, they sent ships to explore the coasts all round the Mediterranean and the Black Seas. These expeditions looked for places where the Greeks could start colonies. The map shows how successful they were.

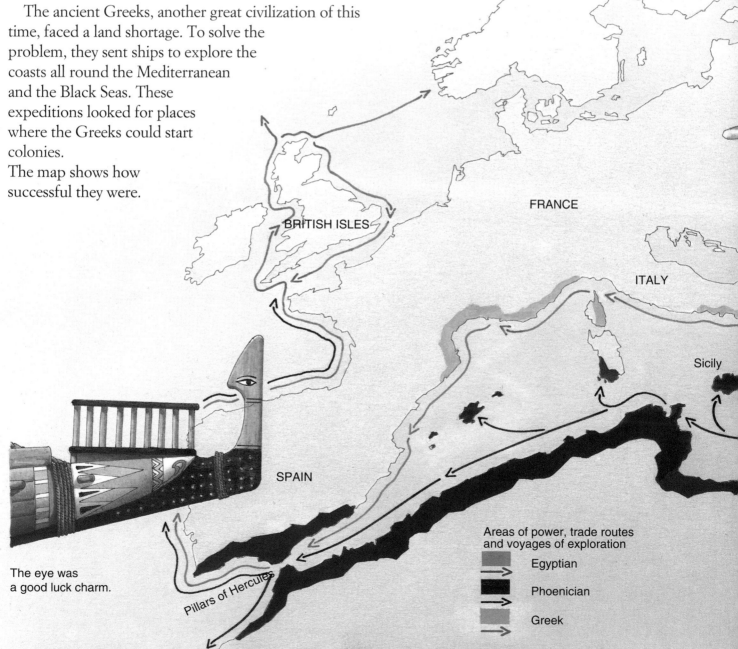

FRANCE

BRITISH ISLES

ITALY

Sicily

SPAIN

The eye was a good luck charm.

Pillars of Hercules

Areas of power, trade routes and voyages of exploration

Egyptian

Phoenician

Greek

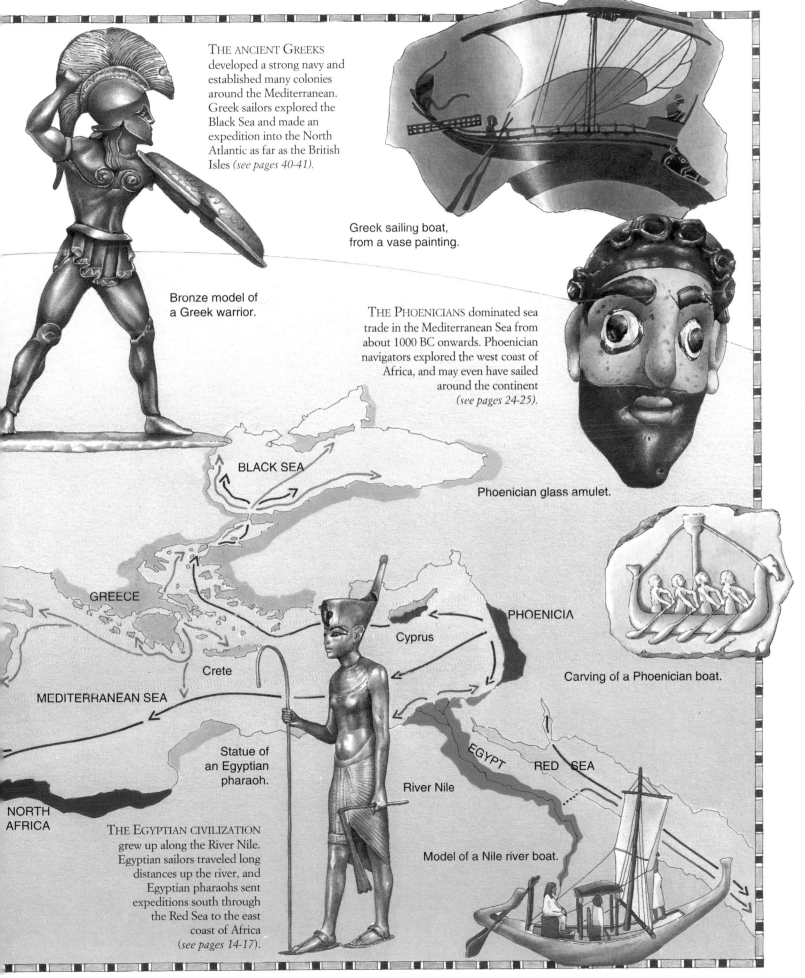

THE ANCIENT GREEKS developed a strong navy and established many colonies around the Mediterranean. Greek sailors explored the Black Sea and made an expedition into the North Atlantic as far as the British Isles *(see pages 40-41).*

Greek sailing boat, from a vase painting.

Bronze model of a Greek warrior.

THE PHOENICIANS dominated sea trade in the Mediterranean Sea from about 1000 BC onwards. Phoenician navigators explored the west coast of Africa, and may even have sailed around the continent *(see pages 24-25).*

Phoenician glass amulet.

BLACK SEA

Carving of a Phoenician boat.

GREECE

PHOENICIA

Cyprus

Crete

MEDITERRANEAN SEA

Statue of an Egyptian pharaoh.

EGYPT   RED SEA

River Nile

NORTH AFRICA

THE EGYPTIAN CIVILIZATION grew up along the River Nile. Egyptian sailors traveled long distances up the river, and Egyptian pharaohs sent expeditions south through the Red Sea to the east coast of Africa *(see pages 14-17).*

Model of a Nile river boat.

7

Egypt and the Nile

One of the richest of all early civilizations was in ancient Egypt. It developed about 3000 BC (five thousand years ago) along the banks of the River Nile. The river was the source of Egypt's wealth. Each year the Nile flooded the surrounding land, covering it with a rich soil called silt. This made the land very fertile.

The river was also ancient Egypt's main highway. It was much easier to travel along the river than risk a journey through the desert that borders each side of the Nile valley.

The river also linked the Mediterranean with the heart of Africa. Rare tropical goods, such as ivory and skins, were shipped down the Nile to Egyptian cities, such as Thebes and Memphis, or to countries beyond.

Some of the boats used on the Nile are shown on these pages.

PAPYRUS PLANTS, flourished along the banks of the Nile. They grew up to twenty feet high. The ancient Egyptians used papyrus to make paper and to build river craft.

Nile Delta

Memphis

RED SEA

Pyramids

EGYPT

Thebes

Temples

THE EARLIEST EGYPTIAN WOODEN boats were similar in shape to the papyrus boats. They were steered with an oar at the stern (back).

Temple of Abu Simbel

BOATS were such an important part of Egyptian life that they were put in the tombs of pharaohs for them to use in the afterlife. The wooden boat of Cheops (above) was made around 2560 BC. It shows how skillful Egyptian boatbuilders were.

HOW PAPYRUS BOATS WERE BUILT

1. The earliest Egyptian river craft had a high stern. Boats like these are still built in the Sudan.

2. As time went on, the front and back of the vessel looked almost the same.

3. Egyptian boatbuilders curved the papyrus reeds over at the stern. Later, wooden boats were shaped in the same way.

River Nile

TO THE SOUTH of ancient Egypt was Nubia. Sometimes it was controlled by the Egyptian pharaohs, but if the pharaoh was weak, the Nubians seized power in their region. Goods from tropical Africa reached Egypt through Nubia, which was also a good source of slaves.

NUBIA

Navigation in Ancient Egypt

The people of Egypt built many different types of boats to take themselves and their cargoes along the Nile. The first boats were made from the reeds that grew on the river's banks. However, by 2500 BC, ships were being made from cedarwood imported from Lebanon (Phoenicia). Wooden boats are much stronger than reed ones. Pharaoh Sahuré, who ruled around 2500 BC, sent sea-going ships to the east African coast.

The Egyptians preferred to travel along the Nile or the Red Sea coast, as navigators could always find their way home.

The weather made travel along the Nile easy. It's current flows north, but a steady wind blows south all year. So, to go south, sailors just kept the sail up. To go north, they lowered the sail and the current and oarsmen did the rest.

WHEN TRAVELING ON THE NILE, with the current, the sailors lowered the mast and the oarsmen rowed.

CARPENTERS used bronze tools to build their wooden boats. No-one had yet discovered how to make iron.

A typical Nile boat of around 2500 BC.

A THICK ROPE was stretched between two posts at the bow and stern (front and back). It tied them together and made the boat stronger.

SIX HELMSMEN, with six large oars, stood at the stern to steer the boat.

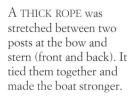

THE OARSMEN could rest when the boat was sailing.

rope

THE EARLIEST VESSELS had masts made of two poles joined at the top.

THE MAST was set well forward, near the front of the boat. It was kept in position with many ropes.

THE CAPTAIN stood at the front, keeping a watchful eye on the river. He guided the boat on a safe course by shouting orders to the helmsmen.

rope

CARGO was stacked on the deck. It was important to keep the weight even, so the boat was stable.

EGYPTIAN BOATS were made by tying the pieces of wood together with rope. When the rope got wet it shrank, pulling the wood together and making the hull stronger.

rope

Hatshepsut's Voyage

One of the greatest of the early voyages of exploration was to Punt. It took place during the reign of Queen Hatshepsut of Egypt, who ruled from 1489 to 1469 BC.

Punt was a land far to the south of Egypt. But, although so far away, the Egyptians knew about Punt through trade. Merchants had been bringing rare and exotic goods, such as incense and myrrh, from Punt for centuries. They brought other things too. Archaeologists have found records describing the Egyptians' excitement when a "dwarf was brought from Punt in the time of King Issi", about 2500 BC.

The expedition to Punt was so important that Queen Hatshepsut had an account of it carved on the walls of her great burial temple near the city of Thebes. And that is the reason we know about it today!

QUEEN HATSHEPSUT reigned from 1489 to 1469 BC. She was the only woman ever to rule Egypt with the full title of pharaoh. This sculpture shows her wearing the pharaoh's crown.

Queen Hatshepsut's temple at Deir-el-Bahri.

QUEEN HATSHEPSUT had a massive burial temple built for her at Deir-el-Bahri, near Thebes. This temple, which stands at the foot of a rocky cliff, had two large terraces reached by long ramps. Two halls with columns along each side contained wall-carvings showing the queen's divine birth and the expedition to Punt.

MYRRH TREES brought back from Punt were planted in the grounds of the temple. *(see page 16)*.

BEFORE THE FLEET DEPARTED for Punt the crew made a sacrifice to the goddess Hathor, "the mistress of Punt". They asked her to "send a favorable wind".

EGYPTIAN CRAFTSMEN made the precious raw materials from Punt and Africa into beautiful objects. This box is made of ivory and ebony.

The Journey to Punt

Five large ships sailed for Punt. They were specially built for the journey at a port at the north of the Red Sea. Each ship was fitted with a huge sail to make the most of every breath of wind. There were also thirty oarsmen to provide extra power. The ships were laden with provisions for the journey, and with goods to trade with the people of Punt. The fleet probably set sail between June and October, when winds blow south down the Red Sea.

We do not know how long the journey took, because we do not know how fast the ships traveled. If they traveled at a speed of 3-5 knots (1 knot = 1.15 mph) and sailed for 12 hours with a good wind, they could travel between 40 and 70 miles a day. Also, no-one knows exactly where Punt was. It may have been a month before the ships left the arid shores of the Red Sea. Sailing ever further south, the Egyptians at last reached Punt – somewhere on the east coast of Africa.

THE MAIN PURPOSE of the expedition to Punt was to obtain incense for use in Egyptian religious rituals. Myrrh trees, from which incense comes, grow in the border area between Ethiopia and Somalia, as well as in southern Arabia.

A HELMSMAN, standing in the stern, steered the ship with two big oars.

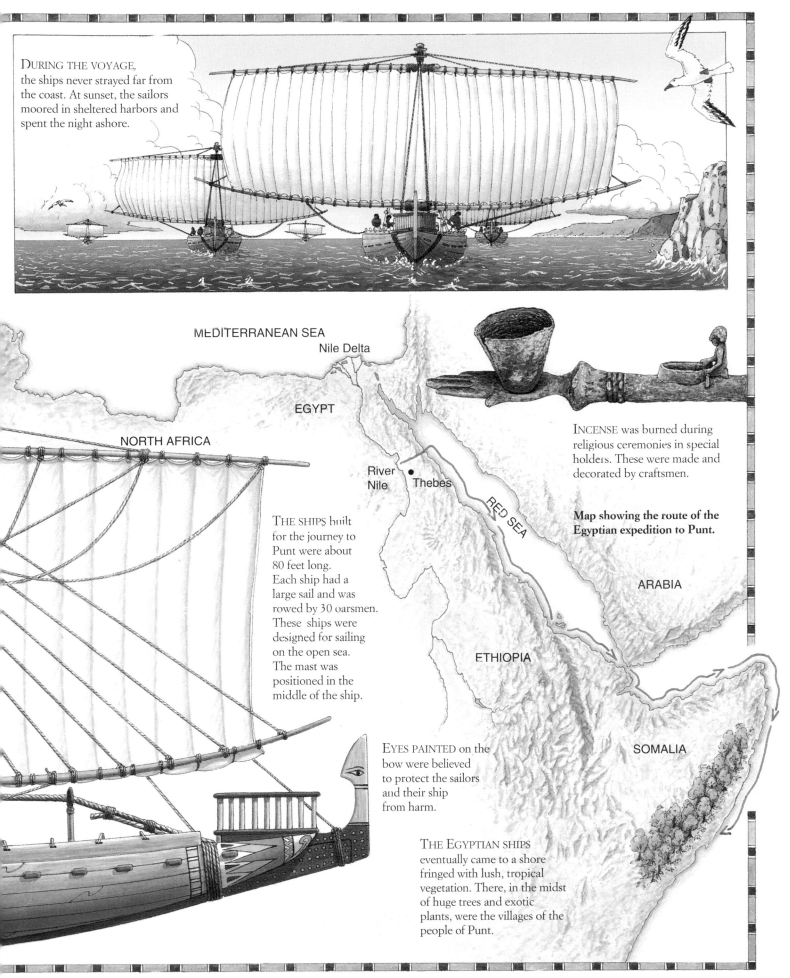

DURING THE VOYAGE, the ships never strayed far from the coast. At sunset, the sailors moored in sheltered harbors and spent the night ashore.

MEDITERRANEAN SEA

Nile Delta

EGYPT

NORTH AFRICA

River Nile • Thebes

RED SEA

INCENSE was burned during religious ceremonies in special holders. These were made and decorated by craftsmen.

Map showing the route of the Egyptian expedition to Punt.

ARABIA

THE SHIPS built for the journey to Punt were about 80 feet long. Each ship had a large sail and was rowed by 30 oarsmen. These ships were designed for sailing on the open sea. The mast was positioned in the middle of the ship.

ETHIOPIA

SOMALIA

EYES PAINTED on the bow were believed to protect the sailors and their ship from harm.

THE EGYPTIAN ships eventually came to a shore fringed with lush, tropical vegetation. There, in the midst of huge trees and exotic plants, were the villages of the people of Punt.

The Treasures of Punt

The Egyptians anchored their ships and went ashore. The ambassador gave gifts to the chief of Punt. After agreeing a price for the myrrh trees and other goods, the Egyptians loaded their ships with the precious cargo. The scene is described in Queen Hatshepsut's temple: "The ships are laden very high with the treasures of the land of Punt, and all the beautiful plants of the Divine Land, with heaps of incense, with great myrrh trees, with ebony and pure ivory, with white gold from Amu, with sweet-scented woods, with all manner of incense and eye pigments, with baboons, monkeys and greyhounds, with skins of the southern panther, and with slaves and their children. Never has the like been brought to any king since the beginning of time."

THE MOST PRIZED GOODS brought back from Punt were thirty-one myrrh trees to be planted in Egypt. The aromatic gum produced by the plant was burned in religious rituals. It was also used as a perfume and for embalming (preserving dead bodies).

1 Good-luck eye
2 Strengthening rope
3 Myrrh tree
4 Leopard
5 Ivory tusks
6 Cage for wild animal
7 Official checking goods
8 Carrying myrrh trees
   on board
9 Steering oar
10 Baboon
11 Axes and daggers

THE PEOPLE OF PUNT lived
in small round huts with thatched
roofs.

IN EXCHANGE
for the riches of Punt,
the Egyptians gave daggers, axes
and beautiful necklaces, as well as
bread, wine, dried fruits and
honey-cakes.

AN EGYPTIAN OFFICIAL
checked all the goods as they
were taken on board each ship.
Baboons and monkeys ran
around the ships during the
return voyage to Thebes.

Bronze Age Trade

The Egyptians did not trade only with Punt. By 2000 BC, during the period archaeologists call the Bronze Age, the eastern Mediterranean was the center of a thriving trade system, linking many of the states in the area. Much of the trade was handled by Canaanite merchants, who came from the coastal lands of present-day Syria and Lebanon. Trade made the merchants rich and the land of Canaan prosperous.

Recently, off the coast of Turkey, underwater divers discovered an ancient shipwreck. The ship, which sank in the 14th century BC, may have come from Canaan. Its rich cargo of raw materials and finished goods has helped archaeologists piece together the jigsaw of Mediterranean trade during the Bronze Age. The map shows how it worked.

Ceramic jars, jugs and two-handled cups were made by Mycenean craftsmen.

BLACK SEA

Baltic amber

Mycenean vase

ITALY

Mycenae

GREECE

TURKEY

Tin ingot

Ivory

Map showing Bronze Age trade routes and the most important goods.

Site of shipwreck

Cyprus

SYRIA

*

Crete

Stone anchor

Canaanite amphora

Ivory may have come from Syria.

Copper ingot

Silver bracelets

Glass ingots

MEDITERRANEAN SEA

A layer of stones laid on the bottom of the ship acted as ballast to keep it steady.

EGYPT

Nile

NORTH AFRICA

Ebony

RED SEA

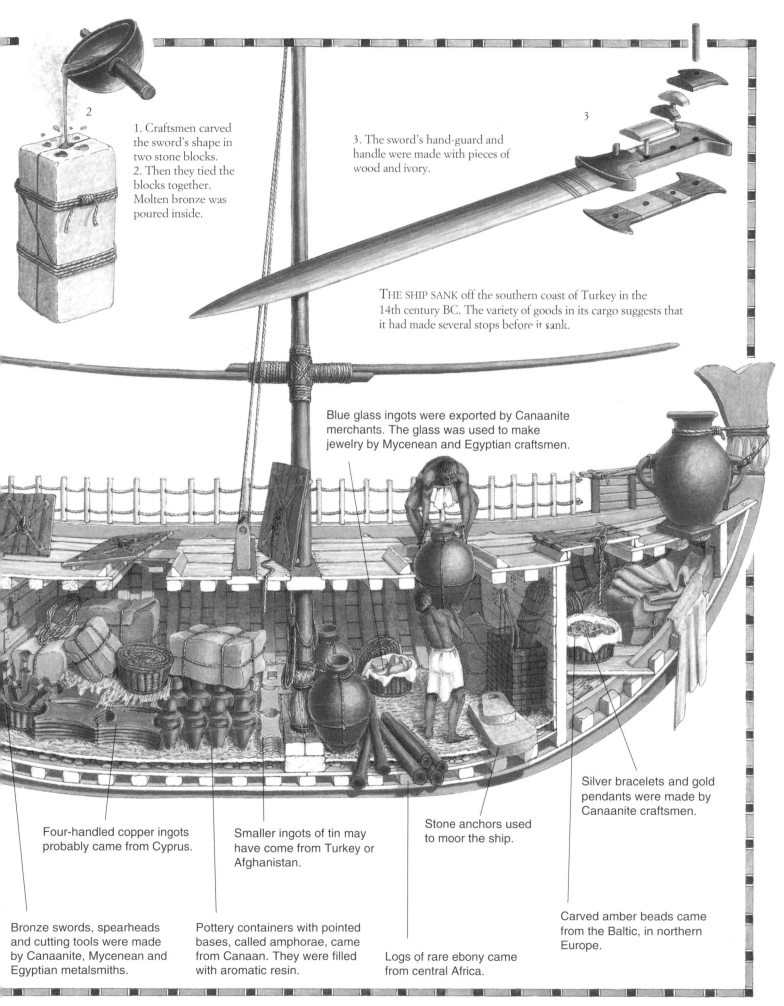

2

1. Craftsmen carved the sword's shape in two stone blocks.
2. Then they tied the blocks together. Molten bronze was poured inside.

3

3. The sword's hand-guard and handle were made with pieces of wood and ivory.

THE SHIP SANK off the southern coast of Turkey in the 14th century BC. The variety of goods in its cargo suggests that it had made several stops before it sank.

Blue glass ingots were exported by Canaanite merchants. The glass was used to make jewelry by Mycenean and Egyptian craftsmen.

Four-handled copper ingots probably came from Cyprus.

Smaller ingots of tin may have come from Turkey or Afghanistan.

Stone anchors used to moor the ship.

Silver bracelets and gold pendants were made by Canaanite craftsmen.

Bronze swords, spearheads and cutting tools were made by Canaanite, Mycenean and Egyptian metalsmiths.

Pottery containers with pointed bases, called amphorae, came from Canaan. They were filled with aromatic resin.

Logs of rare ebony came from central Africa.

Carved amber beads came from the Baltic, in northern Europe.

The Phoenicians

The people of Canaan are probably best known by the name the Greeks gave them several centuries later: Phoenicians.

The territory of Phoenicia (Canaan) was small and the land unsuitable for farming. The best way for the Phoenicians to make a living was from the sea. The forests covering much of their land provided excellent timber for shipbuilding, and the Phoenicians soon became skilled navigators and traders. Strong states, like Egypt and Assyria (in part of modern Iraq), sometimes ruled Phoenicia. But they always let the Phoenician merchants carry on handling shipping and trade. For nearly a thousand years the Phoenician merchants helped build up their country's wealth, while other states rose and fell. But, by about 1100 BC, the Phoenicians were masters of the Mediterranean.

IN THE HARBOR of Tyre a Phoenician *hippoi* (horse-headed ship) is being unloaded. Copper ingots come from Cyprus. Other goods include jars of grain, papyrus rope and rolls of paper, linen and ivory tusks.

TIMBER was the Phoenicians' most important export. Cedarwood was prized because the trees provided long timbers and the wood was strong and long-lasting.

THE PHOENICIANS transported trunks of cedar by tying them behind their merchant ships.

Phoenician ships in the harbor at Tyre.

THIS ANCIENT CARVING shows a Phoenician horse-headed ship with timber.

THE CITY OF TYRE was one of the great trading cities of the ancient world. The city had a fortified wall, houses many stories high and two large harbors.

Phoenician Trade

At first, the Phoenicians just traded in the eastern Mediterranean. Here, the great empires of Egypt and Assyria were within easy reach of their ports. Later, powerful civilizations rose in the west – the Greeks around the Aegean Sea and the Etruscans in Italy. The Phoenicians made longer voyages to develop trade with these powers and to obtain products from further away, like precious metals from Spain.

From the 9th century BC onwards, the Phoenicians began setting up colonies around the Mediterranean. In this way they controlled trade throughout the entire Mediterranean.

The Phoenicians' most important exports were timber and a purple dye made from shellfish (opposite). (The purple robes of the Roman emperors were dyed with this dye.) The merchants also carried goods from other countries: spices from India, and ivory, skins and rare woods from Africa. As well as being successful traders, the Phoenicians were also skilled craftsmen. Their jewellery and glass have been found in many places around the Mediterranean.

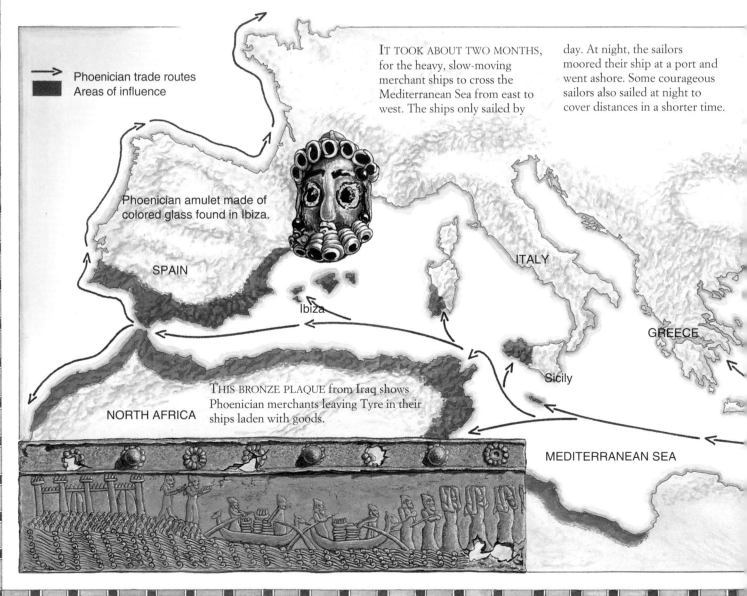

Phoenician trade routes
Areas of influence

IT TOOK ABOUT TWO MONTHS, for the heavy, slow-moving merchant ships to cross the Mediterranean Sea from east to west. The ships only sailed by day. At night, the sailors moored their ship at a port and went ashore. Some courageous sailors also sailed at night to cover distances in a shorter time.

Phoenician amulet made of colored glass found in Ibiza.

SPAIN

Ibiza

ITALY

GREECE

Sicily

THIS BRONZE PLAQUE from Iraq shows Phoenician merchants leaving Tyre in their ships laden with goods.

NORTH AFRICA

MEDITERRANEAN SEA

PHOENICIAN CRAFTSMEN produced high-quality glass objects like these blue vases and pretty necklace.

THIS PIECE OF POTTERY is inscribed with Phoenician writing. The Phoenicians developed a "phonetic" alphabet. This was an alphabet like our own, in which each letter represents a sound. Before this, people (like the Egyptians) used symbols to represent complete words or ideas.

BLACK SEA

KING SOLOMON of Israel (who reigned in the 10th century BC) sent Phoenician sailors to Ophir (southern Arabia, or even India). They brought back gold, ivory, sandalwood and peacocks.

PHOENICIA

Cyprus

Figure of a Phoenician merchant carrying a copper ingot from Cyprus.

A Phoenician ship on a silver coin from Sidon.

EGYPT

THE PHOENICIANS were famous for making a purple dye, which was used to color fabrics in a special dyeing yard. They extracted the dye from a shellfish called murex (right). Tyre was an important center for the preparation of the dye. The name "Phoenicia" comes from a Greek word meaning purple.

Sailing Around Africa

In 600 BC, according to the Greek historian Herodotus, the Egyptian pharaoh Necho II hired a crew of Phoenicians to sail around Africa. Necho was sure that if a ship sailed south down the Red Sea, and followed the coast of Africa, it would eventually enter the Mediterranean from the west, through the Pillars of Hercules (the ancient name for the Strait of Gibraltar between Spain and North Africa). Necho was right, of course, but neither he nor the Phoenicians realized the huge size of the African continent.

The voyage was a success. The Phoenicians completed their journey of 15,500 miles in just under three years. Each spring they went ashore to sow grain and wait for the harvest. After reaping the new grain, they put to sea again with a fresh supply of food. After two years they entered the Mediterranean and in the third year arrived back in Egypt.

We do not know if this story is true, but if it is not, how did Herodotus know it was possible to sail around Africa?

EARLY SAILORS used a simple instrument called a quadrant to calculate their position. The quadrant was a wooden quarter circle, calibrated along the curved side. By looking at the sun or a star through two small holes on one of the straight sides, a lead-weighted thread fell vertically and indicated how far the star or sun was above the horizon. This gave an exact measurement of latitude.

⟶ The route of the Phoenicians

⟶ Winds

⟶ Currents

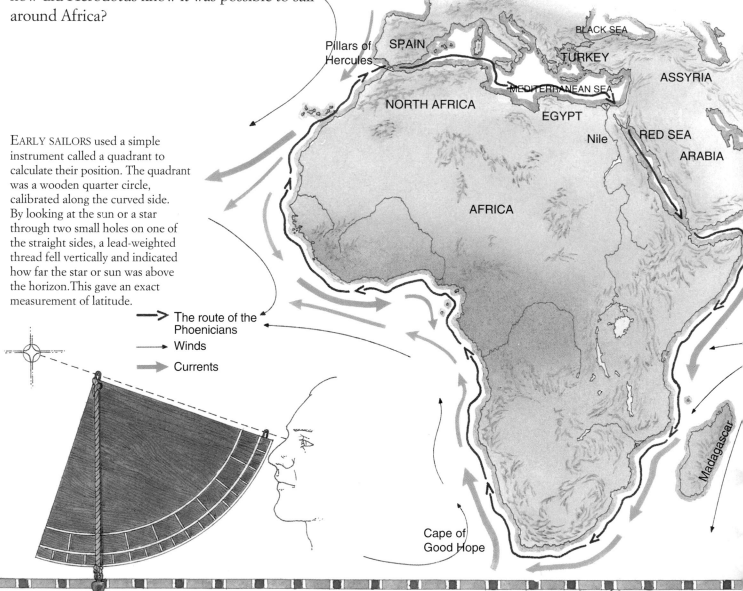

THE BIG SAILS on the Phoenicians' ships caught even light breezes. Sailing clockwise around Africa meant the Phoenicians were helped by many winds and currents, as the map opposite shows.

One of the Phoenicians' ships rounding the Cape of Good Hope, the southern tip of Africa.

Phoenician Colonies

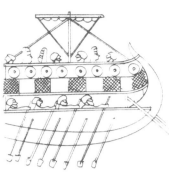

The Phoenicians set up many colonies in North Africa, Spain and on the islands of Sicily and Sardinia. Most of these colonies were trading cities which also controlled an area of coast. The most famous colony was Carthage, in modern Tunisia, founded around 814 BC by settlers from Tyre. Carthage flourished and quickly became the most powerful Phoenician colony in the Mediterranean. The city controlled trade in the western Mediterranean. For centuries its navy guarded the Strait of Gibraltar, preventing ships from other states sailing through. Carthage became the base for important voyages of trade, exploration and colonization beyond the Mediterranean Sea. By 600 BC the Phoenicians had founded a small trading colony at Mogador, 600 miles south of Gibraltar on the African coast. In the 5th century BC, Hanno, a Carthaginian admiral, led a famous expedition along the west coast of Africa. (*see pages 28–31*).

The shipyards at Carthage in the 5th century BC.

THE PORT OF CARTHAGE was made up of two parts. An outer harbor, with direct access to the sea, was used for merchant ships. An inner, military port was used only for warships. In the middle of the military port was the admiralty, surrounded by the shipyards where the warships were built.

Mediterranean Sea

harbor for merchant navy

admiralty

harbor for warships

THE PHOENICIANS used longships for war and long-distance trade and exploration. Each ship had a single sail and two banks of oars. On either side of the high stern was a steering oar. In battle, warriors hung their shields along the sides. Underwater, the ship had a pointed bow which was used to ram enemy ships in battle.

THE SHIPBUILDERS USED rope pulleys
to haul the heavy timbers into position.
They slung the ropes over the ceiling
beams and tied them to rings
in the stone pillars.

THE CARTHAGINIAN ADMIRAL,
Hanno, studies the model
of a ship in the shipyard
at Carthage. Behind him, several
ships are being built.

The Voyage of Hanno

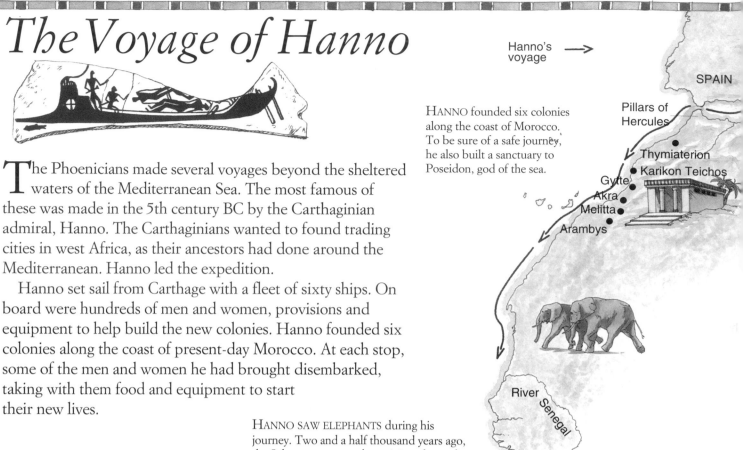

The Phoenicians made several voyages beyond the sheltered waters of the Mediterranean Sea. The most famous of these was made in the 5th century BC by the Carthaginian admiral, Hanno. The Carthaginians wanted to found trading cities in west Africa, as their ancestors had done around the Mediterranean. Hanno led the expedition.

Hanno set sail from Carthage with a fleet of sixty ships. On board were hundreds of men and women, provisions and equipment to help build the new colonies. Hanno founded six colonies along the coast of present-day Morocco. At each stop, some of the men and women he had brought disembarked, taking with them food and equipment to start their new lives.

HANNO'S voyage →

SPAIN

Pillars of Hercules

HANNO founded six colonies along the coast of Morocco. To be sure of a safe journey, he also built a sanctuary to Poseidon, god of the sea.

Thymiaterion
Karikon Teichos
Gytte
Akra
Melitta
Arambys

River Senegal

HANNO SAW ELEPHANTS during his journey. Two and a half thousand years ago, the Sahara was not as dry as it is today and these animals roamed areas which are now desert.

HANNO stopped to trade with natives along the coast. Leaving their goods on the beach, the Carthaginians returned to their ships and raised a smoke. The native people then laid gold beside the goods and retired to a safe distance. This was called the "silent" trade. It continued until the Carthaginians were satisfied with the "price" offered.

HANNO'S FLEET included many merchant ships. These were used to carry the goods that were bought during the journey.

ITALY

GREECE

MEDITERRANEAN SEA

PHOENICIA

Carthage

Nile Delta

NORTH AFRICA

hara Desert

The Carthaginians trading with a group of native people.

Exploring the African Coast

After leaving the last of the settlers, Hanno continued his voyage southwards. During this journey into uncharted waters and along unexplored coasts, he saw many strange and wonderful sights. He sailed long distances up rivers and saw many strange animals. During one such excursion, Hanno described being attacked by wild people dressed in animal skins. At another point along the coast he was frightened away by the eerie sound of beating drums and voices yelling in the night. Towards the end of his journey, he met "people completely covered in hair"!

We do not know exactly how far Hanno traveled. But from his description of tropical shores it seems that he may have traveled along the west coast of Africa as far south as the Gulf of Guinea.

Hanno exploring the River Senegal.

WITH TWO SHIPS, Hanno sailed up a river which was probably the one now called the River Senegal. On each bank were dense forests, full of strange trees with sweet-smelling wood.

River Senegal

HANNO and his crew saw a volcano erupting, sending torrents of lava into the sea.

THE RIVER swarmed with crocodiles and hippopotamuses.

AT NIGHT, Hanno saw blazing lights on the plains. These were probably grass fires which broke out in the dry season.

THE CARTHAGINIANS encountered hairy savages, probably baboons or chimpanzees. Three were killed and their skins taken back to Carthage.

Gulf of Guinea

31

Greek Colonies

The mainland of Greece is rough and mountainous. It is not good for farming. As the population grew, people looked for more land to settle. From about 750 BC, many Greek cities sent out colonists to seek new homes overseas.

The Greeks founded hundreds of colonies. They settled on the numerous islands in the Aegean Sea, along the coasts of Turkey and Libya, and around the shores of the Black Sea. Other colonists headed west. Soon there were so many Greek colonies in southern Italy and eastern Sicily that the area was called Magna Graecia, which means "greater Greece". Further west, the Greeks founded colonies along the coasts of France and Spain.

The colonies quickly became independent states with their own rulers. Temples, theaters and other monuments were built. Artists, scientists and philosophers lived in the colonies and so helped to spread Greek culture far and wide.

A GREEK SOLDIER. The Greeks spread their influence through colonies and culture rather than war.

THE NAMES of some Greek colonies have survived until the present day. Naples was the ancient Greek city of Neapolis, which means "new city".

GREEK CITIES were well-planned. The street plan of Miletus, a Greek colony on the west coast of Turkey, shows the streets running parallel to each other and crossing at right angles.

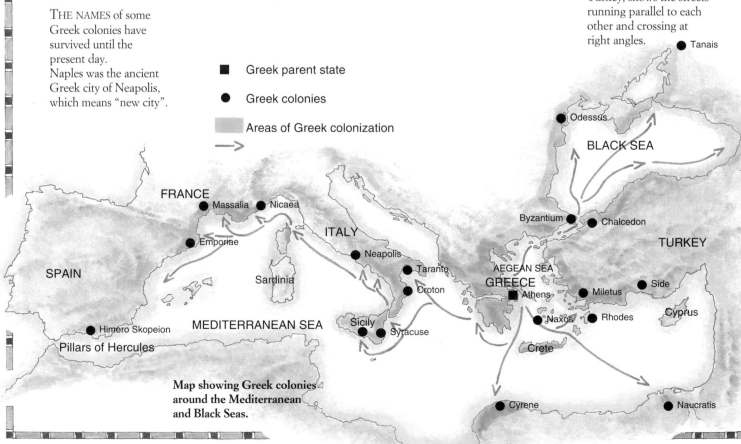

- ■ Greek parent state
- ● Greek colonies
- ▨ Areas of Greek colonization
- →

Map showing Greek colonies around the Mediterranean and Black Seas.

SPAIN — FRANCE — Massalia — Nicaea — Emporiae — ITALY — Neapolis — Taranto — Croton — Sardinia — Sicily — Syracuse — Himero Skopeion — Pillars of Hercules — MEDITERRANEAN SEA — GREECE — Athens — AEGEAN SEA — Naxos — Rhodes — Miletus — Side — Crete — Cyprus — TURKEY — Byzantium — Chalcedon — BLACK SEA — Odessus — Tanais — Cyrene — Naucratis

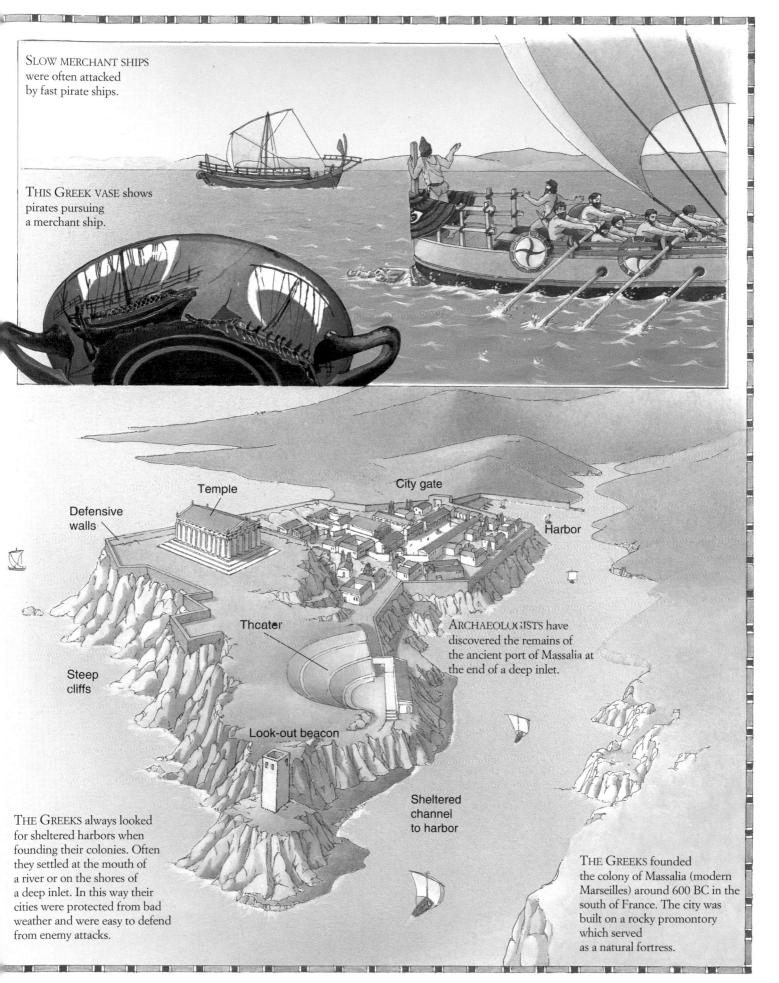

SLOW MERCHANT SHIPS were often attacked by fast pirate ships.

THIS GREEK VASE shows pirates pursuing a merchant ship.

Temple

City gate

Defensive walls

Harbor

Steep cliffs

Theater

ARCHAEOLOGISTS have discovered the remains of the ancient port of Massalia at the end of a deep inlet.

Look-out beacon

Sheltered channel to harbor

THE GREEKS always looked for sheltered harbors when founding their colonies. Often they settled at the mouth of a river or on the shores of a deep inlet. In this way their cities were protected from bad weather and were easy to defend from enemy attacks.

THE GREEKS founded the colony of Massalia (modern Marseilles) around 600 BC in the south of France. The city was built on a rocky promontory which served as a natural fortress.

A Journey to the Black Sea

The Greeks wrote long poems about the adventures of many mythical heroes. One famous story describes the voyage of Jason and the Argonauts. Jason sailed to Colchis, on the eastern shores of the Black Sea, to capture the Golden Fleece. If Jason accomplished this difficult task, his evil uncle, King Pelias, would give his kingdom to Jason. The story of Jason and his voyage is a legend. But it is probably based on real events. Greek colonists settled the coasts of the Black Sea in the 7th century BC, but they may have explored them centuries earlier. The Greeks certainly obtained gold from the Scythians, a nomadic people who lived in the steppe-lands north of the Black Sea.

ACCORDING to the Roman geographer Strabo, the Scythians trapped gold particles by pegging sheepskins to the beds of shallow mountain streams. When the sheepskin was put into a fire, the wool burned, the gold ran out and was easily collected.

BLACK SEA

Caucasus Mountains

→ Jason's voyage

Bosphorus

Colchis

GREECE

AEGEAN SEA

TURKEY

Crete

MEDITERRANEAN SEA

THE MAP shows the areas of Greek settlement around the Black Sea. Colchis, where Jason sailed to find the Golden Fleece, was near the Caucasus Mountains, where the Greeks obtained gold from the Scythians.

Jason and the Argonauts in their ship, the *Argo*.

IN THE 4TH CENTURY BC Greek craftsmen molded the gold into fine jewelry, including these rams' head bracelets.

TO REACH THE BLACK SEA, the Greeks sailed through a turbulent channel called the Symplegades. Today it is called the Bosphorus.

Falling rocks threatened to sink Jason's boat as it sailed through the rough waters of this channel.

The Port of Piraeus

The Greek colonies grew rich from trade. They competed with each other, and at times fought battles with enemy powers, like the Phoenicians of Carthage or the Etruscans of Italy. To protect their merchant ships, the Greeks started building warships.

By the 5th century BC the Greeks had a fleet of warships strong enough to defeat the might of the Persians. Athens alone had 200 triremes, manned by about 40,000 men: sailors, oarsmen and soldiers. The port of Athens was at Piraeus, a fortified center on the coast some 6 miles away. Warships and merchant ships were built and repaired there. Every day, when the weather was favorable, many ships set sail from Piraeus. They brought back grain from Egypt, metals from Spain and the Black Sea, and slaves from Africa and northern Europe.

PERICLES RULED ATHENS during the 5th century BC, which is sometimes called the "golden age" of Athens. He strengthened the city's navy to protect shipping and trade routes.

PIRAEUS was a small city. As well as its three harbors and houses, there was a large square and two theaters.

The port of Piraeus in the 5th and 4th centuries BC.

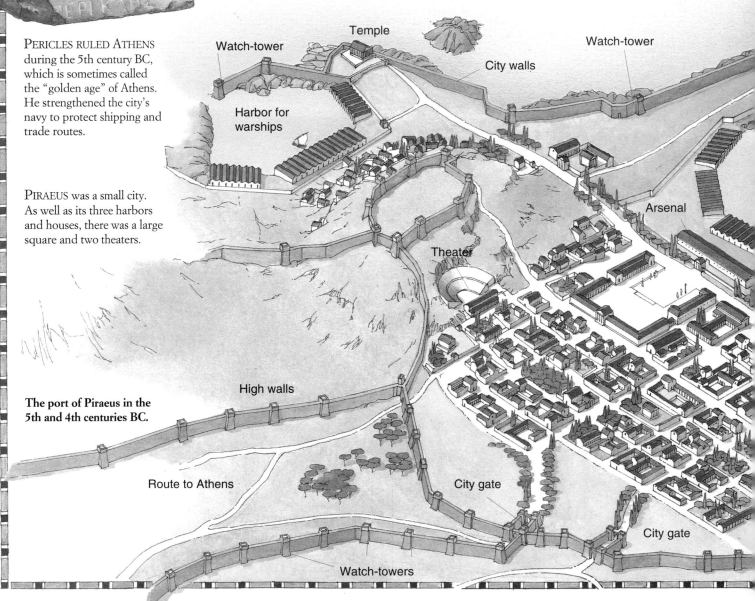

Watch-tower · Temple · Watch-tower · City walls · Harbor for warships · Arsenal · Theater · High walls · Route to Athens · City gate · City gate · Watch-towers

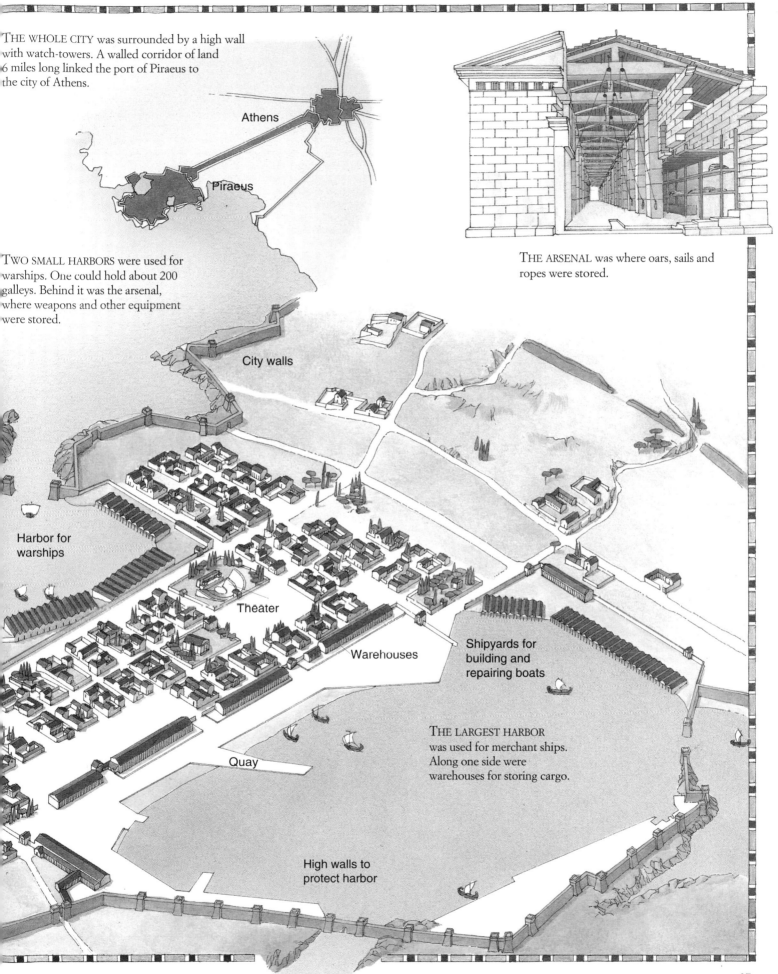

THE WHOLE CITY was surrounded by a high wall with watch-towers. A walled corridor of land 6 miles long linked the port of Piraeus to the city of Athens.

Athens

Piraeus

TWO SMALL HARBORS were used for warships. One could hold about 200 galleys. Behind it was the arsenal, where weapons and other equipment were stored.

THE ARSENAL was where oars, sails and ropes were stored.

City walls

Harbor for warships

Theater

Warehouses

Shipyards for building and repairing boats

THE LARGEST HARBOR was used for merchant ships. Along one side were warehouses for storing cargo.

Quay

High walls to protect harbor

Greek Ships

The Greeks had two types of ship – merchant ships and warships. The Greek merchant ship was called a holkas. It needed a strong hull with plenty of space for storing goods. It was therefore a broad, heavy ship, which relied mostly on wind power and traveled slowly. Because it was so heavy, it was rowed only when absolutely necessary.

The most important warship in the 5th and 4th centuries BC was the trireme. The trireme needed to be fast and easy to maneuver. Its long, slim shape meant that it could move swiftly through the water. The trireme was rowed by many oarsmen. In battle, the oarsmen could turn the ship quickly and sink enemy ships with a powerful thrust of the trireme's underwater ram.

Conditions on warships were very cramped. But merchant ships had enough space to carry passengers, as well as cargo, and could travel for several days across the open sea.

THE GREEK WORD "trireme" means "three oars". These ships had three rows of oarsmen, one above the other, on each side. The top row of oarsmen sat in a special "outrigger". They had to row harder because they were higher above the water.

THE TRIREME was about 130 feet long and 16-20 feet across. It was normally rowed by three rows of oarsmen (170 men) and could reach speeds of up to 10 knots (11½ mph).

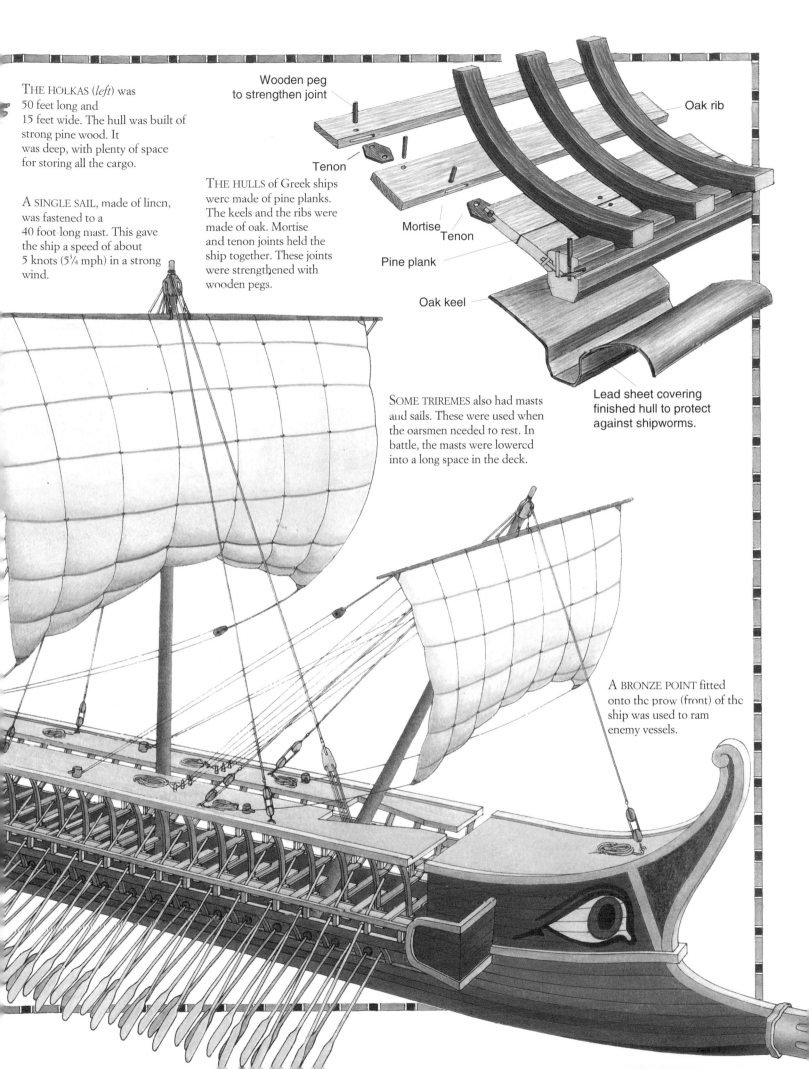

THE HOLKAS (*left*) was 50 feet long and 15 feet wide. The hull was built of strong pine wood. It was deep, with plenty of space for storing all the cargo.

A SINGLE SAIL, made of linen, was fastened to a 40-foot-long mast. This gave the ship a speed of about 5 knots (5¾ mph) in a strong wind.

THE HULLS of Greek ships were made of pine planks. The keels and the ribs were made of oak. Mortise and tenon joints held the ship together. These joints were strengthened with wooden pegs.

Wooden peg to strengthen joint

Oak rib

Tenon

Mortise

Tenon

Pine plank

Oak keel

Lead sheet covering finished hull to protect against shipworms.

SOME TRIREMES also had masts and sails. These were used when the oarsmen needed to rest. In battle, the masts were lowered into a long space in the deck.

A BRONZE POINT fitted onto the prow (front) of the ship was used to ram enemy vessels.

The Travels of Pytheas

In the 3rd century BC a Greek scientist called Pytheas made a famous voyage into the North Atlantic. Pytheas was born in Massalia, a Greek colony on the south coast of France (now Marseilles), which was on an important trade route. The Celtic peoples of northern Europe brought raw materials to Massalia to be traded throughout the Mediterranean.

The purpose of Pytheas's journey was to go directly by sea to the source of tin, which was mined in Cornwall.

Pytheas sailed from Massalia around the Iberian Peninsula (modern Spain and Portugal) and north as far as Brittany, stopping regularly to take on water and provisions. He then crossed the English Channel to reach the densely forested land of southern Britain. Sailing westwards along the coast, he finally saw the many tin mines which covered the hills of Cornwall. He had reached his goal.

PYTHEAS was the first navigator to realize that the Iberian Peninsula has a roughly square shape. When he sailed into the Bay of Biscay Pytheas measured his position and found he was at the same latitude as Massalia.

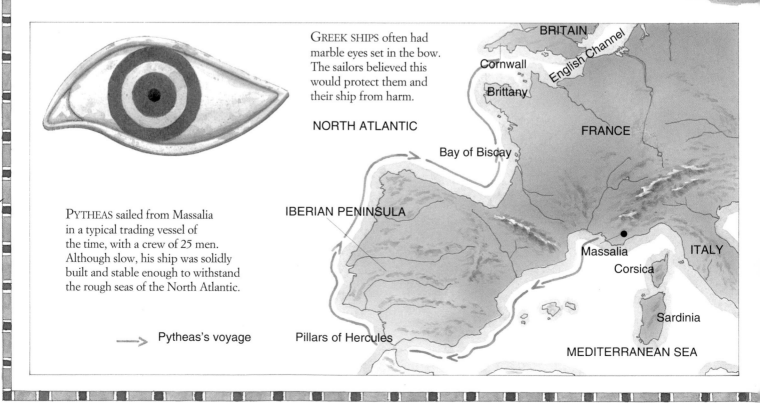

GREEK SHIPS often had marble eyes set in the bow. The sailors believed this would protect them and their ship from harm.

PYTHEAS sailed from Massalia in a typical trading vessel of the time, with a crew of 25 men. Although slow, his ship was solidly built and stable enough to withstand the rough seas of the North Atlantic.

NORTH ATLANTIC

BRITAIN

Cornwall

English Channel

Brittany

Bay of Biscay

FRANCE

IBERIAN PENINSULA

Massalia

Corsica

ITALY

Sardinia

Pillars of Hercules

MEDITERRANEAN SEA

→ Pytheas's voyage

Cornish miners transporting ingots of tin.

THE MINERS loaded the tin onto waggons and transported it to an island, not far from the shore (present-day St. Michael's Mount in Cornwall). They could only do this at low tide, when a causeway was uncovered. Sea-going merchants came to the island to obtain the tin.

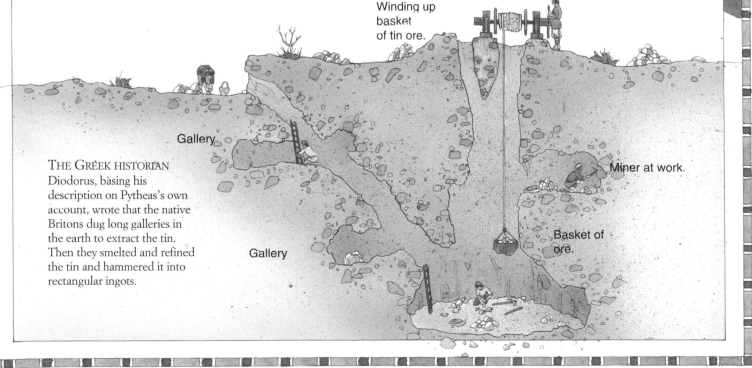

Winding up basket of tin ore.

Gallery

THE GREEK HISTORIAN Diodorus, basing his description on Pytheas's own account, wrote that the native Britons dug long galleries in the earth to extract the tin. Then they smelted and refined the tin and hammered it into rectangular ingots.

Gallery

Miner at work.

Basket of ore.

The Voyage to Thule

After visiting the tin mines of Cornwall, Pytheas continued his voyage northwards. He sailed through the Irish Sea, exploring the many inlets along the west coast of Britain. He described the native Britons as a friendly people, but noted that the climate was horrible! He observed how the forests of southern Britain gradually gave way to moorland and pasture, and eventually to the barren rocky landscape of northern Scotland.

Pytheas sailed through seas far rougher than those of the Mediterranean. Yet in spite of this, he ventured even further north, until he reached a mysterious land called Thule. Here, dense fog and ice-filled seas turned him back.

Pytheas wrote an account of his travels, but the book was later lost. We only know about his great voyage from other people who had read his book.

PEOPLE LIVING around the Mediterranean found it difficult to believe Pytheas's description of the Sun that never set (right). At mid-summer the Arctic Circle has sun all day long because the Earth is tilted towards the Sun, which does not go below the horizon.

→ Pytheas's voyage

AFTER CIRCUMNAVIGATING BRITAIN, Pytheas sailed eastwards to the west coast of Denmark. Here he visited Samland, the source of amber. Amber, which was greatly prized in ancient times, was traded throughout the Mediterranean. It was often made into jewellery like the bracelets (left).

Iceland

Thule?

Faeroe Islands

Shetland Islands

NORWAY

Thule?

SCOTLAND

Irish Sea

DENMARK

Samland

BRITAIN

Cornwall

NO-ONE KNOWS where the mysterious land of Thule was. Pytheas said that the Sun never set in summer. This means that it was certainly somewhere near the Arctic Circle. Perhaps Pytheas reached the Faeroe Islands, or the Norwegian coast, both lands of the "midnight sun".

Pytheas sailing through the ice-bound waters of Thule.

PYTHEAS made many interesting discoveries on his journeys. Voyaging along the coasts of northern Europe, he observed the movement of the ocean tides. He was correct in thinking that tides are linked to the phases of the Moon. The Moon's force of gravity attracts things toward it just like the Earth's. Although it is weak compared to the Earth's gravity, it is still strong enough for it to affect the oceans over 238,900 miles away. This force of gravity "pulls" the oceans on the Earth's surface producing movements of the sea which we call tides. The highest tides are at or near a full Moon when the effect of the Moon's gravity is at its greatest. The lowest tides are when the Moon it in its first or third quarter and the Moon's effect is at its least. Pytheas did not know it but over 70 percent of the Earth's surface is underwater.

The Geography of the Ancient World

In early times, people had different ideas about the size and shape of the Earth. The ancient Egyptians believed that the Earth was flat and rectangular, with four massive pillars at each corner holding up the heavens. The ancient Greeks thought of the Earth as a flat disk, surrounded by an endless stretch of everflowing ocean. The maps on these two pages show how three early geographers visualized the world.

The first person to declare that the Earth was a sphere was the Greek philosopher Pythagoras in the 6th century BC. About 150 years later, Aristotle, another Greek philosopher, showed this was proved by the curved shadow of the Earth on the Moon during an eclipse. Later, a Greek scientist called Eratosthenes made a very accurate calculation of the size of the Earth.

However, in spite of their scientific discoveries, the people living at this time still knew very little about the world outside the Mediterranean. For many centuries to come, for example, people thought that beyond Europe, Africa and Asia, the rest of the Earth was covered by one vast ocean.

The maps of early geographers.

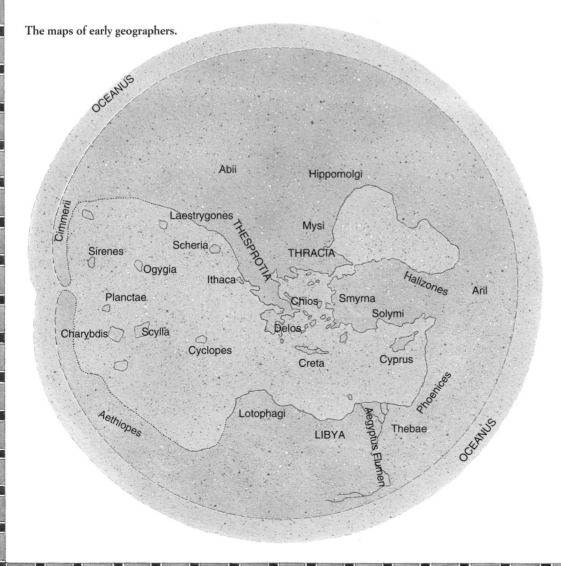

THE WORLD OF HOMER (ABOUT 700 BC).
Homer is the author of the Greek epic poems *The Iliad* and *The Odyssey*. He put Greece, and the islands of the Aegean Sea, at the center of the known world, surrounded by an endless stretch of sea called Oceanus. The coasts of the Mediterranean Sea are not very accurately drawn, but the River Nile, the Black Sea, and the Strait of Gibraltar are all recognizable.

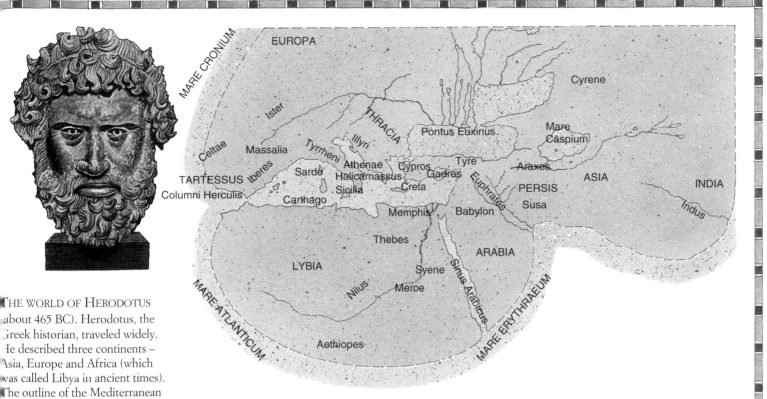

THE WORLD OF HERODOTUS (about 465 BC). Herodotus, the Greek historian, traveled widely. He described three continents – Asia, Europe and Africa (which was called Libya in ancient times). The outline of the Mediterranean is much more accurate, and many rivers and towns are marked. Africa is shown surrounded by sea, except where it is joined to Asia.

THE SAILORS OF ANCIENT TIMES made long voyages of exploration without the help of sea charts and accurate navigational instruments. Where possible, they sailed along coasts. The Mediterranean Sea has many peninsulas and scattered islands, which meant that even if sailors ventured into the open sea, land was never far from sight. Sailors also oriented themselves by the position and movement of the sun, the stars, the winds and sea currents.

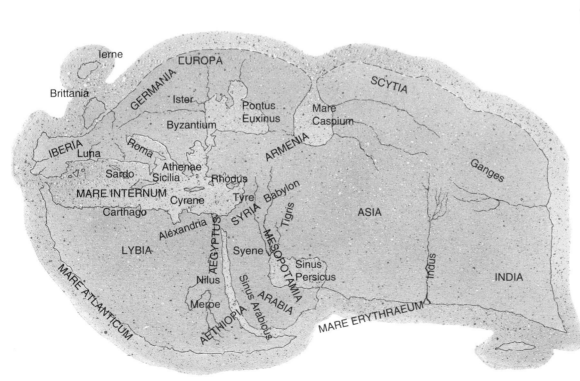

THE WORLD OF STRABO (about 25 BC). Strabo was a Roman geographer. As the Roman Empire expanded, so the boundaries of Europe became better known and more accurately mapped. However, the Caspian Sea, really a huge lake, is wrongly shown joined to the sea.

TIME CHART

EGYPT

BC
c. 3500 Invention of the sail.
c. 3400 First defended towns in Egypt.
c. 3100 Pharaoh Menes unites Egypt; builds capital at Memphis. Papyrus boats are used on the Nile.
c. 3000 First evidence of hieroglyphic writing.
c. 2560 The Great Pyramid of the Pharaoh Cheops is built. The boat of Cheops is built.
2500 Sea-going sailing ships are built. Early expeditions to Punt.

1652 Egypt at war with the Asian Hyksos peoples.
c. 1560 Nubia is conquered.

1489 Queen Hatshepsut comes to the throne.
c. 1485 Queen Hatshepsut's expedition to Punt.
1323 King Tuthankhamon is buried.

1367 King Akhenaten rules and begins new religion.

1166 Death of Ramesses III, the most powerful pharaoh of Egypt. From this time on, Egypt's power slowly declines.

GREECE

BC

2600 Early Minoan period in Crete.

1700 New palaces built in Crete.

c. 1600 Mycenean civilizations begins.
1450 Eruption at Thera and the end of the Minoan civilization.

1250 Mycenean forces attack the city of Troy in Asia Minor (Turkey).
c. 1200 Mycenae ceases to be a powerful city-state.

1150 Mycenae is destroyed.

1000 Mainland Greeks begin to emigrate to Asia Minor (Turkey).

776 First Olympic Games.
c. 750 Greek city-states begin to found settlements along the Mediterranean and Black Sea coasts.
Homer writes the epic poems *The Iliad* and *The Odyssey*.
c. 700 The Greeks develop trade with the Scythians.
550 Sparta at its height of power.
c. 530 Pythagoras, the philosopher and mathematician, states the Earth is a sphere.
508 Democratic government formed in Athens.
c. 500 First triremes built. Population of Athens is 250,000.
490 Birth of Pericles. Defeat of Persians at Marathon.
480-340 The Golden Age of Greece. Great achievements in art, science and philosophy.
447 Building of the Parthenon begins in Athens.
431-404 Peloponnesian War between Athens and Sparta, won by Sparta.
336 Alexander the Great becomes King of Macedonia.
c. 250 Pytheas of Massalia sails to the British Isles.

GLOSSARY

PHOENICIA & CARTHAGE

c. 4000 Bronze casting begins, probably in the area of modern Iraq.

c. 3000 Cedarwood is exported from Byblos to Egypt for shipbuilding.

2000-1550 Canaanite culture flourishes.

1550-1150 Canaan is dominated by Egypt, but Canaanite merchants control trade in the eastern Mediterranean. Glass-working is developed.

c. 1200 Decline of power of Cretan and Mycenean peoples. Phoenician cities take over trade in Eastern Mediterranean.

c. 1100 The Phoenicians develop an alphabet. Rise in power of independent cities of Tyre, Byblos, Beirut, Sidon and Aradus. Discovery of Spain's metals.

c. 950 Fortified city of Tyre built by King Hiram. Phoenicians, in the pay of King Solomon, sail to Ophir (India?).

814 Phoenicians from Tyre found Carthage.

666 City of Tyre taken by Assyrians.

650 Carthage becomes the most powerful Phoenician city.

600 Phoenician sailors, hired by the Pharaoh Necho II, sail around Africa.

c. 450 The Carthaginians reach the British Isles and buy tin.

c. 425 The Carthaginian admiral Hanno explores the west coast of Africa.

Amber
the hard, yellowish, fossilized resin of extinct coniferous trees. Used to make jewelry.

Amulet
a trinket or charm worn to ward off evil.

Aromatic
sweet-smelling.

Ballast
heavy material, such as stones, used to make a floating vessel stable.

Beam
the width of a ship at its widest.

Bow
the front of a vessel.

Causeway
a raised path crossing water.

Helmsman
the person who steers at the back of a boat.

Hull
the main body of a boat or ship.

Incense
an aromatic substance burned for its sweet smell, used in religious ceremonies.

Ingot
a piece of metal that has been molded into a regular shape.

Keel
the central timber that runs along the bottom of a boat, from bow (prow) to stern.

Latitude
the distance in degrees north or south of the equator.

Mycenae
city-state in ancient Greece.

Myrrh
an aromatic plant which produces a resin used in perfumes and incense.

Outrigger
a projecting framework attached to a boat.

Pigment
a natural substance used to make a color.

Prow
the bow (front) of a vessel.

Raw materials
materials (like metal, wood or clay) which are processed to produce finished goods.

Sacrifice
killing an animal and offering it to the gods to obtain their favor.

Silt
a fine deposit of mud in a river.

Smelt
to extract a metal from its ore by heating.

Steppe
wide, grassy plains.

Stern
the rear part of a vessel.

Trireme
Greek warship of the 5th-4th centuries BC, with three banks of oarsmen.

INDEX